While the Bells Ring

While the Bells Ring
William Mayne

Illustrated by
Janet Rawlins

Hamish Hamilton

First published in Great Britain 1979 by
Hamish Hamilton Children's Books Ltd.,
Garden House, 57–59 Long Acre, London WC2E 9JL
ISBN 0 241 89932 x
Printed in Great Britain by
Ebenezer Baylis and Son Limited
The Trinity Press, Worcester, and London

For Court,
who has been here

ONE

I smelt the cut grass when I woke. It was still right early, and I think it wakened me. Our Jane Ann was below laying the fire, and Lizbie was asleep yet. I got up out of bed.

"Cover me up again, Kitty," says Lizbie. I pulled up our big quilt. It was that early the pattern looked all black, when it was red and blue by day. Lizbie sucked on her thumb and hunched under the covers like an urchin.

I went on down. "Get the cows home," says our Jane Ann. "We's haytiming."

"I ken that," I says. "Is it breakfast in the grass today?"

"No," she says, and she was cracking a match in the fire and I could see the white smoke in the black chimney.

"He's mowing our little garth and he'll be done by we've milked."

The sun was up better than a crack when I got outside, and all the field walls caught the light and held it off the ground. The cows were down in the bottom by the lakeside. It was just roky on the water and I couldn't see across it. But there were folk awake at yon side, for our cows turned and looked across, and a moment after I heard it too, Patersons calling of their cows. So ours get called in too, and come my way, and get milked.

When we had the milk in the dairy Jane Ann goes up to get Lizbie down, because we never had a mother since Lizbie was born and Jane Ann does the most part in the house. I went on down to our little garth to ask our Dad whether Jane Ann is to mash the tea. I ran on down the lane, to keep my feet out of the meadows, which are ours one side and Paterson's the other.

"Why, aye," says our Dad, "she can do that. I've but a little bit to do, seest tha, and I'll be home. Did you milk?"

"All done," I says; "and the cows in the middle lake pasture."

"Right enough," he says, and went on sharpening the scythe. He had his coat hung on the gate, and two or three buttons of his waistcoat loosed, and a fly or two already hung round his head. In front of him there was the tall grass along the bottom of the garth, and behind

6

him it was all mown off and laid in snod rows and the sun shining off the stems brighter than the scythe blade. "I'll soon wallop off yon," he says; and he put the stone in his belt and swung the blade again and it sighed through all the stems and toppled them.

I began to run back home then, but I stopped by the gate a moment, because there was Bram Paterson coming up the lane leading a horse and the horse was pulling a mowing machine. Bram could come to such an expense. It came trolling on behind the horse, making the biggest clatter and wrangle, and I could feel its iron wheels tread the ground.

I don't know where he is going, or I could have opened the gate for him; but it was better not to, belike, because it was never square-aways between him and Dad. So I stood a bit, and our Dad mowed on without looking up; and Bram might not have seen me stood there in front of him, but turned in the gate aquart of ours and went into that garth, where the machine ran faster.

He wasted no time; the blades began cranching the grass at once, and Bram's away, ten times as fast as Dad, as quick as the horse went.

Then I ran home and told our Jane Ann to wet the pot.

That was all the haytiming for that day, either side of the lane. Our next piece wasn't ready to mow, and what was cut had to kill and dry before we could get it in. But there's always summat to be done, and the same sun would

7

dry the winter bedding for the cows. It was hard days on and light days off in haytime.

So the afternoon times then we would be out on the lake along our side in the reed boat with Dad knelt in it scything under the water, and us lifting up the bundles and laying them in the boat. Mostly it was me and Lizbie, with Jane Ann at our landing with Sugar, our horse, and a cart, leading the reeds away and strowing them in the top pasture to dry like the hay.

One of those afternoons we cut a bit, and drifted a bit, and Jane Ann on the land sat up again a rock, and Dad and I were telling Lizbie them old stories about the lake, and the old pilgrim that got it put there, and Lizbie was looking down in the water and saying she could see a roof and a tower and a road and people, and hear the church bells, which they say you can see and hear one time or another, belonging the people who never gave the pilgrim shelter so he cursed the water over them. That was the day Bram came out on a rock his side the water and dived in and swam about and then climbed out on the rock

8

again. Out he came, and all his back as he goes up is white like a candle, and then when he turned his front is black as coals, his dark beard not stopping at his neck but growing all down his chest, all fur to his knees.

"Black Bram," says Dad. "That's what they call him. Black Bram. Well, we've done nowt today; we'd better go back and milk the cows." Black Bram pulled on his breeches and went home, and so did we.

Then the next day we had the little garth to turn, to kill the grass underneath, and we had to be on with that; and over the lane there was Bram and his mother and an Irishman all turning their field. Turning is turning, to this day, and we went along the rows and tipped the dry under and the green on top, and the rake handle pulled my hands up in blebs and then rived the skin off the blebs. Dad went on and on up and down the garth, but Jane Ann did hab and nab of my rows amonghands with hers until she saw I wasn't framing so well, and she came up and dropped her rake and wiped my eyes with her sleeve and looked at my hands.

"Now Kit," she says, "it's too hard for you and you must stop for a bit and we'll put some milk on those sores."

So we both stopped, because it was time to get the dinner ready, and stopping was as bad as going on because then my own sweat and some of my own tears got on my hands and made them swidge worst of all. I didn't know

10

I was so daft-handed.

Black Bram looked over his wall at us as we went by. His shirt was open and his chest was a great black fleece. Well, I looked at him, but he never looked at me, so he looked at Jane Ann.

"Was your skirt rid up, or summat?" I says when we had gone up the lane a lile bit. She just gave me a thump and told me not to be so common-like.

My hands mended and we got on grandly with the hay, though we had only three of us, my Dad and me, and one lass, Jane Ann, working, with Lizbie big enough to play, that was all. So we did that garth and had another cut before it was in, and worked our way round. But wherever we went, and there were not many fields to our farm, there was Black Bram working in the next one. Our Dad saw it first off, but the way the land is we have Paterson's on one side of every garth, so when we were in Beldin Bram was in Delveland, and when we were in Fairy Haw he was in the Hull, and when were in East Micklefarthing he was in West Micklefarthing, and when we were in Grain Sike he was in Grain Beck. Our Dad didn't like being so followed, but there was nowt he could do. Bram had but to look out over the lake and see where we were working and he would come over. If it was cutting he might have to trail the mower right round the lake from end to end, but it could take him half a day and he would still be mown off before my Dad. If it was turning or dashing or the rest of that, then he and the Irishman would come over in their reed boat, bobbing over in a minute.

It was one thing knowing where Bram was; but there was a day or two when he wouldn't appear; there would just be the Irishman working on his own. I didn't notice, but it was clear after that those days our Jane Ann wasn't always in sight neither. They said nowt, Jane Ann and my Dad, but there was summat up, and by, he could do nothing right, she got that patched of her temper, I never knew she could be so twined.

There came a day when it was to rain, so we left the cut grass and led in the pikes we had. The hay goes in jockeys first, like an armful twice, and then gets put in pikes to stand the weather, and our Lizbie slid down them all day. Jane Ann and Dad could tip a pike on the sledge and Sugar would pull the sledge to the mew and Dad fork the hay up in the forking hole and me and Jane Ann would take it in. Our Dad went back for more pikes and Jane Ann forked the hay up and I threw it back.

That day there was Jane Ann up with me and the hay still coming in, and down below was Black Bram on the hay and hoisting it up until it was all in, and Jane Ann jumped down from the mew and he caught her, and looked at her from close by. But then Sugar knocked on a stone and I heard the spurs of the sledge on the ground.

"Away," says I for warning, and Bram goes away, and we finished the pikes alone.

TWO

We had some glishy days then, when the sun would shine a bit and then there would drop a shower, and it was bad to tell what to do with the hay, whether to leave it as it lay or turn it and get it wet again. But we got at it by habs and nabs, and got pikes up in Beldin with a sheet on them to turn the rain.

The weather was the same on Black Bram and the Irishman, but they got away at the job better. They had to turn by hand, but for cutting they had the mower, for dashing they had a dasher with spiked wheels to throw the hay up and scatter it, and they had the horse rake to draw over the field and make windrows. We had all to do by hand.

14

"You had a lend of the horse rake last year, Dad,"
says Jane Ann. "And there it is in Delveland idle."

"Thou can never borrow for nowt," said Dad. "I isn't
off to get in the debt he wants me in. We must work on
by ourselves."

But he couldn't do without some help coming his side
of the wall, for not long after, when we were making
jockeys between showers, there came climbing the wall
the Irishman, with his rake and a hay fork. Our Dad
stopped work and waited of him.

"I see you're not very friendly with your neighbours
this year," says the Irishman. "The time was when we'd
be sharing the work."

"That was another year," says Dad. "Not this."

"Then it's for old times' sake I'll give a hand here,"
says the Irishman, "and for yourself and the pretty girls."

"Take no heed of them lasses," says our Dad. Jane Ann,
she smiled for the Irishman, and Lizbie jumped about and
says she'd rather marry a Scotchman, but she was only a
little lass, and Jane Ann calls her a bessy-babs and made
her cross.

It was a big help, the Irishman, until he went, and our
Dad says he thanks him but it goes no further; he won't
thank Bram Paterson.

The weather got out later, and we went well with
Fairy Haw, but with Bram in The Hull alongside, and
then we left that for a day and went to East Micklefarthing.

15

Then I thought that Bram might not be working alongside us by plan, because he wasn't in the West Farthing, and I could hear him raking over in another place. But he came in the West Farthing towards night, with not much to do there, and stood against the wall watching us a bit while we dashed the hay. Then he went off and dashed the West Farthing.

We went on home for milking time, right on towards dark it was, and Lizbie fallen asleep in the hay so we had to find her, and I hiked her up and carried her, and she had her fingers in her gob and slothered on my neck.

We came by Fairy Haw, and Dad took a look over the gate at the hay, and Jane Ann with him.

"That wasn't the fairies," says Jane Ann, in a strange hoping voice.

"I wish it was," says our Dad. "They're better folk to deal with than yon."

But I was glad, whoever did it, when I looked through the gate and saw what Bram had been doing: going over our field with the horse rake, leaving it all windrowed ready to push up in pikes. But it wasn't right for me to say so, and when I did Dad opened up and told me Bram had no right in our fields and on our hay, even if he thought it. I know Bram has some rents or owings from us each year, but that's money, not hay, and then I didn't see that one might be the other, and that even the land might go, until Dad says how Bram might be stepping forward of his claim.

"He did it to help," says Jane Ann.

"Never," says our Dad. "Never." And Jane Ann swallowed down her words and her thoughts and we went on for the cows.

I took Lizbie up and put her in the bed. My eyes were so tired they kept dropping closed, but I went down again and milked part and kindled up a fire, and our Dad kicked off his boots before it and supped his tea and I fell asleep on the stobbed rug our Mam made in the time I remember. So I went up to bed, and Jane Ann came just after me, and I was going to ask her what made her cry but a shiver came up my back and sent me to sleep.

We cracked on hard the next day and we got Fairy Haw piked up, and we led the pikes out of Beldin and put that up in the mew over the shippon. That was all the hay we had at home; the rest we put in the lear up on Grain Sike.

B

Of course Bram knew what we did, and so he was up at Grain Sike before we got up with the first pike from Fairy Haw.

He went up on the baulks, the upper floor, and we lifted hay up there. First I was up and taking the hay back, and then he came forward and none of them saw down below that he was forking in. I never thought, but in a bit I went out down the steps and began to help down below, and if our Dad had looked he would have seen straight off there were three below and none above, but he didn't look. After a bit he went off with Lizbie leading Sugar for another pike, leaving us with what we had to put in. So we put in until it was all gone and then Jane Ann climbed up the wall on the rough stone and got her head level with the floor above, where the forking hole door is, and Bram lay on the floor where he can see her and see out, and just put his hand over the sill to touch her fingers, and they don't say a word, and by, it is quiet while Sugar comes back.

I went up the steps and passed hay back to Bram, until I found myself outside again and being handy turning Sugar round. Then our Dad looked round and counted us up, Lizbie down by the sike, me turning Sugar in the top pasture, Jane Ann beside him shifting hay; and another fork up in the mew that was none of ours.

"We'll just do what we have," says our Dad, quite gently, "and we'll be off home while Monday. I's just off

18

up to latch the forking-hole door, and we'll ride down on the sledge."

So he went up the steps, when we'd forked in, and in at the door. But before he was at the top we heard Bram drop down the fothering hole into the hay-rack in the buse below, and Jane Ann loosed the shippon door and he came out and went off down the hill towards the lake, and I thought he was running away.

Our Dad came down again, and never said a word; but he would know what was going off and he would be

thinking what was to be done. But all we did now was get on the sledge and ride on down. Dad looked at Sugar and Jane Ann looked at the ground going by, and Lizbie tumbled off the sledge and then ran after it shouting and bauling because she runs against it and hurt her leg because she can't go slow enough to keep off. I looked down the fields and saw Bram dodging across our lands down to the waterside, and I didn't wonder why, but thought I wouldn't venture towards fighting with our Dad, and it isn't as if Bram was any younger, being just the same age, and a black hairy belly won't make him stronger only looking so. Then he came to the lake shore and went into the water and swam right on across and away up the other side to Paterson's.

No one said a word our side but Lizbie, and we took no gaum of her because we all had something else between us that wasn't words.

"I'll bath them little ones," says Jane Ann, in a bit.

"I'll bath in the lake," says our Dad, and I knew he hadn't looked at Sugar's backside all the time but had seen Bram go down and cross the water and knew where he was, out of the way.

Bram wasn't so much out of the way as we supposed. I thought he had run off but that wasn't it. I was in the tub in front of the fire with Lizbie, and Dad was down at the lake, and Jane Ann was in the dairy when he came back.

20

Lizbie saw him coming by the window. "Man," she says, and hopped up out of the tub and went to the door, reached up, and opened it.

"Now then, honey," says Bram, "is thy Dad home?"

"I am that," says our Dad, and he just came to the door behind Bram. "What dost want, Bram? Kitty, come and take Lizbie back in the water and tell our Jane Ann to stop in the house." But I stopped where I was, felted away under the water and shy to get out.

"We'll be outside then Bram," says our Dad.

"I'd sooner be in, for this," says Bram. "Thou knows."

"Then it'll ha' to be the front room," says our Dad.

"It'll ha' to be the front room," says Bram. "That's the start of it, I think, Rich." That was our Dad, Rich Armistead.

"Aye," said Dad. "I can say it inside or out, Bram, between thee and me," and they go through the room and our Dad dropped Lizbie in the tub again and Jane Ann watched from out of the dark door of the dairy. And she stepped back and skelled over the evening's new milk, every drop and said nowt, and we said nowt, and we heard nowt from the front room, for the door was fast shut. And I thought I would never be brazzen-faced enough to go in a house and ask a man for one of his lasses, in case I got no for answer, like Bram would.

THREE

Jane Ann shut herself in the dairy instead of coming to fetch Lizbie out of the water, so I did that, and then there was nowt to do but go up to bed. Jane Ann shouted back at us when I went to the dairy door, and I felt too ashamed of Bram getting told no to go in the front room and see him at it.

But when I got into bed I began to hear it all in the room below. I thought Bram should be out by now, because our Dad would say no and that would be it. Happen it's a longer word than it looks, is no. I sat up in the bed and told Lizbie to get to sleep, and I listened through the floor without trying.

". . . and that's the first end on't," says our Dad, at the finish of something.

"Thou has taken it wrong," says Bram. "What for else would I come?"

"Not for owt thou has talked of, Bram," says Dad. "Thou wants to cross the lane and get a foot in our lands, aye, and then both feet, and then all of thysen; thou's wanting in here, Bram Paterson, and I's not letting thee in."

"Nay, Rich," says Bram, "thou has it wrong. I want but one thing from thee and nowt else. I'd be glad to forget all the money debts between us, Rich, and give above that."

"Shaff," says Dad, like you might say rubbish, "I'll not buy and sell my own kith and kin. Yah time and all times, Bram, there's nowt here for thee."

"Eighteen years since," says Bram, "there was a lass that chose thee before me, and I've said always I'd wait of Jane Ann, and I've thought on, Rich, and what isn't her mother in her is thee, and I wouldn't find better."

"But it isn't to be, Bram," says Dad. "I's not agreeable, and I shan't be, while the bells ring."

If you are a down-country person reading the last my Dad says you might take the meaning wrong, because you would have said "until the bells ring," but up Vendale we say "while the bells ring," and we mean the same thing. The bells are the ones in the city drowned under the lake; and our Dad says "never" when he says that.

"Aye well," says Bram, "I'll not ask again, seest thou."

"Thou'lt not get nigh enough," says Dad, "neither to me nor the bairns."

"I's warning, not offering," says Bram. "I'll find my own road out, Rich."

So that was the end of that. They moved about down below, and I heard Jane Ann say some words to Dad and she came to bed and humped down in the covers and looked at the window while I fell asleep, and maybe longer.

Sunday next day was a moderate drying day so we lost nowt doing nowt. But it was a black day for tempers and strangeness in the house, our Dad not civil to any of us, Jane Ann going about all set in the face so stiff she couldn't speak, and Lizbie maunging on all day for that Jane Ann wouldn't laike on with her, and our Dad wouldn't stir to speak, and I felt it all like it was prickly clothes and maybe I was worst of all. Even Jem our dog got out of the road.

We should have gitten ourselves to chapel in the day but that hung on Jane Ann having all ready, and she never did. So the day trailed on while teatime, and then, when we had that our Dad says: "I's right I know, and we shall have no more to do with Patersons. If you meet them in a lane then step into a garth; if you meet them in a garth then get out on the moor; if you meet them on the moor then come away by to the lakeside; if you meet them on the lake get home."

"Black bad Bram," says Lizbie.

"Whisht," says our Dad. "And what's thou trembling for, Jane Ann: it's nowt to do with thee."

"Aye, marry, nowt in the world," says Jane Ann, and there was tea spilling from her cup her hand was so canty. I didn't see then that she might care one way or another where she lived and in what house. I thought she could be sent or kept and never mind; it hadn't come to me that she would care for Bram just when he cared for her.

In the morning, or maybe the next morning again, but soon, when I brought the cows in to milk there was one with a bit of band round its horn, and I wondered what Lizbie had been at: our cows was that soft and Lizbie that daft she could have ridden them. So I never thought, but Jane Ann went to it at once when she came in the shippon and took off the band and there was a paper under it that she read words on.

"Well," she says, "what for are you looking at me like that, thou great fond thing? Dost think the cow sent me a letter?"

"No," I says, because it came clear to me then. "I think Bram Paterson sent it you."

"Well, Kitty, I'll have to trust you," she says.

"Nobody says you'd not to speak to a cow," I says, because I never thought what was to come next, and when it came I don't know that Jane Ann had thought about it

26

either, the way she went on with it.

Maybe there came more messages. I never looked. But the time went on and we got the last hay in from Grain Sike, with Bram down in Grain Beck watching all, and maybe there was the Irishman at a row end now and then helping on, and maybe there was Micklefarthings part

27

dashed for us and Grain Sike windrowed. But we had the last pike up before tea one day and finished clashing on for the year.

We had our tea, and Jane Ann got out the tub and had the set-pot hot and ready.

"I's off to have a big bath," she said. "You can all get away outside or off to bed, I don't care, but I want the fireside, and I'll be a right long time, like a lady, and if there's any water left when I've done you can join of it, or not, just as you like."

Well, it was like a big preparation for nothing, but we all went in the front room and had a fire in there while she finished. But we never thought what she was to do.

We heard her finish and go upstairs and walk about dressing, getting the press open and taking out and shaking, and we heard her run the window up after a bit, and then there was a scrammling and a call out, and it was quiet, just for the noise of a horse in the yard.

"That's never Sugar," says our Dad. "Who is it then?" So we went out at the back of the house and into the yard, and there's the bedroom window staring open, and down the yard just beyond the gate, and closing it, was Bram on one of their horses, dressed up proud, and pillion at the back of him was our Jane Ann, and it was daft the way she held on round Black Bram's body with her arms and shrieked out with her mouth for help, and for Dad to get her away.

28

"What the Divil do you want?" shouts Bram, just ready to open the gate and put her back again.

"Go on before I stop," says Jane Ann. "Go on, Bram; Dad, help, he's taking me off with him, oh help, get me away," and if she meant it as much as she says it why didn't she hit at Bram instead of slapping the horse across the backside to make it hurry on?

Bram finished getting the gate fastened. "I said I'd not ask again," he calls back. "But thou'll ken where she's at; she can bid wi' my mother a bit. Away lass, stop your bauling."

Our Dad stood and watched. Lizbie began to howl with the fuss and excitement of it, and I didn't know what I was to do, with Jane Ann wanting two things at once.

"Aye well," says Dad, "she'll be back. Let her have her ride out. Just for now we'll get the tub emptied, Kitty."

But first we watched Bram and Jane Ann go off down the lane, and heard her yell, but it was like the dog's bark when it's telling a lie and you can tell it's so. Jane Ann never meant it much; but she didn't sound either that she meant it when she told Bram to hurry on. I could make nowt of my sisters, and there was Lizbie wanting to be off with them and all. They went down the lane and across the bridge at the foot of the lake and then up the road on yon side.

Then we emptied the tub. Next night our Dad went

over there in the reed boat. "Wait by the fire for us," he says. "I don't want you bairns taking the candle about, and you can have Jem in with you. I don't know how long I'll be."

I don't know how long he was. Lizbie and I fell asleep by the fire, and she won't remember but I do, being carried up the stairs to bed.

In the morning there was no Jane Ann.

"Did she land?" I says to Dad.

"No," he said. "We'll have to get her back another way; she's locked up over there and I never saw her and never got in the house. But I know what we'll do, but I'll have to let Bram do his haytiming first for that's before all up here. And I mean no harm to the Irishman. Thou'll be a man like they were in the old days, Kitty, before the summer's out."

"And I'll be a lady," says Lizbie.

"Thou'lt have to be," said Dad. "Thou'lt have a houseful of folk in a week or so, and all to cook for, Lizbie."

That night wasn't the last we got left alone. It wasn't the first, either, but before we always had Jane Ann and now we had just Jem our dog. But that night when our Dad went for Jane Ann and she never came was the longest time he left us before the big night.

The cows missed our Jane Ann as much as any of us. She was a good milker, and she got the butter prize at the show once over for little lasses, when she was a bit bigger than me, but that's work for a lass. But the cows wouldn't thrive after she went, not the same, and maybe the most milk we ever had was what Jane Ann skelled over in the dairy the night Black Bram came asking of her. After that the milk dwindled. I think I might make a farmer, but I'd need a lass like Jane Ann. My own way with cows doesn't seem to please. Our Lizbie was no better yet, and then she gave up on the milking after she got tipped off the stool with a side kick, and I reckoned she was tickling over much.

Our eating wasn't so good, either, in any manner. We had a dowly do of our meals, with our Dad not making neither end nor side of the cooking, and it was getting so our Lizbie would stop outside rather than come in to eat, and I don't know, but I think she lived on currants out of the dairy.

But maybe all that was no long time. I know the fog was growing, the grass that comes after the mowing of the hay, and the cows went in to our little garth first out of the middle lake pasture, and I remember going down alone for them when our Dad was away on one of those days, and it was the day the cows went in Beldin that the first man came because we put his horse in the west lake pasture and it went and stood in the water and I thought its shoes would get rusty. The man laughed, and went away up to the house and I thought I'd maybe said summat daft.

Christopher Awling was the man, and I thought he was a hunter, with his gun on his shoulder, because hunters come on the lake in the back end of the year, and our Dad keeps a big gun, bigger than Christopher Awling's. But this Christopher is no hunter at this time of year, but my cousin some way, and the one I get my name after, because Kitty is Christopher. I don't recollect what he thought of me, for it wasn't me he came to see. Our Dad went off to do a bit of walling and he went on to help.

Next there was Brindley, who wasn't so much of a cousin but some sort of kin, and we knew him from being bald and a bit fresh with drink and having to lie by the wall and sleep and never helped with one stone.

"He's drunk, maybe," says our Dad. "But never daft with it."

They came quicker after that, and Lizbie heard the next one coming up the lane a right long way off and I wouldn't believe her and then I heard it myself, and it turned out to be two horses, and it was the two Copstone Gill men with red hair, our Mam's cousins or the like. Well, we had four horses then by the lake, none of them tied by the house so they weren't come for a short time but a long one, and our cart shed getting full of saddles and our front room filling with guns, for they all come like hunters.

There was another one coming before the Copstone Gill lads got settled, and that was Tan Hill Jack that never said a word and maybe he had no mouth, just closed folds drooping under his nose. He went on up to the walling, but the Copstone Gillers stopped a long while and laiked with Lizbie like she was a play-toy.

Then there's Alice John, coming with his cart and that old square horse of his, but he's bringing nowt, only stopping like the rest, and the Copstone Gill lads laughed

34

at his gun and say he might wing a barn with it but nowt smaller, and of course it's nowt again their smart ones.

Then there's Tommy John, a right pleasant little farmer man from up dale and he was once a soldier and he had a soldier gun but no horse, he walked all the way and Alice John says he should have had a ride up in the cart, and the Copstone Gill lads say that they hope no one rides down in it, and that made them merry.

The Doctor came next, but he wasn't a doctor at all, just a man that's a real cousin to our Dad and he went round the markets and fairs with bottles of jollop, and he had a shooting pistol and I did want it and when they went up to the walling I lifted it off the table and I thought I could shoot a duck with it, or a rabbit, just so, and steady, and bang.

Then the last one came, Billy Mecca, and he was the oldest and he was the only man I ever saw wearing a wig out in daylight, just as a fashion. He was the ninth, and he took his horse up to the walling and I showed him the way.

They had the gap up and were leaning on it and looking over to Paterson's, and that was what they came for, and it was them our Dad kept those long late hours to see. And this night, maybe, and for all the nights it took, they were going over to Bram's and they had the guns and the men to get back our Jane Ann.

So I told Lizbie, and that got her right happy again, but she was twined when we came down to the house and no Jane Ann was there, and she would have nowt to do with the Copstone Gill lot, and not so much to do with me, and there wasn't any of the others had owt to say to her.

36

Alice John had brought plenty of food out of the market, and the Doctor brought four of his big bottles but it wasn't the label that counted this time, he says, so they drank his jollop with their teas, and it was a party and there was a fine fire, and Lizbie got all the fuss ever and I ate myself out and went and milked.

When I came in they were all in the front room and all ladening their guns with what went in. Some you ladened from the end and pack down with a rod, and measure the powder and tip in shot, which takes a time. Others they could laden with a cartridge, but there are two sorts of them: one cartridge you could buy complete at the shop and then the rest of it is no use after the shot; the other sort some of them had, which were like our Dad's for his long gun, brass on the sides and you filled it with powder and shot and put it in the breech of the gun, and the gain of that is you could get several ready and take them with you and fire oftener. Tommy John got a brass cartridge for his gun with one long bullet in it that would kill an ox five garths off, he says. Alice John had a gun, which they all laughed at, ladened with all sorts like nails and bits of stone. And the Doctor got his pistol in another country and he said he could fire it six times without stopping and that was too good for this country where people did not know, but fine the other side of the sea. But I thought it might hit whatever side of the sea you were, if that was where the Doctor was with it. And our Dad ladened his long gun but took out the rabbit gun. The long gun had cartridges ready, but the rabbit gun used shop cartridges.

So that was it. They took up their guns, laid more turf on the fire for me and Lizbie; our Dad fetched Jem in to keep an eye on us, and they went off just when it was

38

coming night.

They never left us a candle, and then it got real dark and I lit a candle-end but it was an inch long and soon went out, and the turf left us in the dark.

I didn't feel very brave by then, and Lizbie says she doesn't like it, and Jem growled a bit but he won't say what for.

Then Lizbie hears it, and I hear it, that there's shouting and calling going on far off, and we don't like it, either of us. So I opened the door, and held Jem so that he couldn't get away, and listened and the black wind breathed on us and the sheep called, and a horse whimpered.

"That's all," says I. And we were going in, and then I heard the voices shouting, and I heard glass breaking, and I heard someone get hurt, and a stone against a wood door, perhaps, and all coming across the lake, from Paterson's.

Lizbie didn't like that and began bauling, and Jem growled again. And I didn't like it either, not knowing what it was and thinking if our lot can go across and do that then Bram and his lot can do the same, and it was no good remembering that our lot have lived in the dale for so long I can't remember, and that Bram's lot just came no time ago at all and couldn't gather kin to join of a fight; no good remembering that, because I could think they might be outside at the windows now and could come in and kill Lizbie and our dog that's trained, and me.

39

So I went fumbling through with Lizbie, in the dark, and I could just see my way, and I fetched a stool and got up again the wall and lifted down the long gun, and I felt better. And I got a cartridge to put it in the breech but there was one ready in, and I closed the gun up again, and I wondered if I could fire it because it was too heavy for me to hold, and I thought that Lizbie could have an end on her shoulder. But I didn't know where to fire it in the house, and I thought we ought to go outside with it, and Lizbie continued to shout and yell and scream for Jane Ann, and I thought we should go across to where she was and be ready and safe for when she came out, and maybe help too.

FIVE

They must have ridden round the lake, I reckoned, so that
meant Lizbie and I had a better way to go. She gave up
bauling a bit when we got across the yard, but she began
again when she stood there while I got the gate unfastened,
because it was so dark. They had taken both lanterns.
Jem our dog stopped in the house, for he never liked to
go out this end of the night. Well, I didn't like to go out
so very well, either but I was force put, and Lizbie
wouldn't side up without I did.

She quietened off when we went down across our lake
pastures and down to the landing. It was a less darkness
now, and I could see fairly, and Lizbie, she walks on owt

41

day or night and it made not so much difference to her. At our landing there was our reed boat with plenty of rainwater in but no help for that. Our Dad would dry it out with his hat. The only thing is not to get the long gun wet, so I gave Lizbie the cartridges to hold on, and laid the gun across the boat, and I was right glad to put the weight down a bit.

Then I'd to pick at the rope-knot in the dark before we got off, and then we loosed of the land, and it hadn't been warm on it but it was right cold off it, starvation it was, and the water jauping again our feet and getting in our boots.

And next we were blind, for I was never a right sailorman rower and I had to look across my shoulder to see where I was going. I remember when our Dad ploughed out Beldin to reseed the meadow and he drove on forward with the plough to a mark he set his eye on the wall and the furrow came right, but I watched the furrow and got nowhere at last. Well, it was the same now; I'd nothing to work to for getting to Paterson landing, back or forth, and then there clapped down a roke on the water and if there ever was a mark it had gone, and I don't know the furrow I rowed. Then we got in the reeds, and they weren't our reeds for our reeds had getten themselves cut, so I was away and I knew we had crossed the lake, and the only thing was, had we got down to the foot of the lake and would we go under the bridge, because a lad once got drowned with that, but it was a hundred years since. There was land to see, like to know it was darker than nowt would be, and I went along one way, and got to Paterson landing and tied up our boat next to theirs, and we'd got across.

Then I had a do with Lizbie, she wouldn't get out of the boat before me, and she wouldn't get out after, and she dropped a cartridge in the water and lost it, and I couldn't lift her out at the same time as myself. But we got off at last both together, and I got down in again for the gun and we trailed up the path to Paterson's.

I don't know that I thought what I was at by then. I'd got Lizbie off bauling, and when I was out in the open on the land there was nowt to be feared, but I had been afraid on the water. But here we were, and I had neither mind nor meaning in it. I just got worrying what our Dad would say and hoping I would do summat brave.

We just came up a pasture to a stee, where you climb the wall, and I was on the step of it when I looked ahead and there's a fellow in the next garth again the house, light enough to see him but dark enough not to tell who it was. So I dragged the gun up ready, and I don't know what I thought, that it might be Bram and he would get Lizbie next if he wanted our lasses, and I don't know what the gun did, but it jumped up in the air and it upscuttled me and gave me a kick in the ribs and a wap on the face and dropped me on top of Lizbie, and I fancy

43

it went off but I heard nowt but a dog bark in the house, and then another gun, and I knew the long gun had fired by the smell and by it was warm. And a dog barked further off, maybe Jem, and another gun, and then a good many, and each time a window comes clattering down at Paterson farm.

Then our Dad comes shouting round, because he knew his own gun sound and came to see what happened, and there's one or two with him and they didn't know what to do with us.

So they stood there and clattered on about it for a bit, and all the dogs for ever round us howled.

"It's a queer do there isn't a dog near the house here," says Tan Hill Jack, I think, but it was dark and I never saw his mouth move.

"By," said our Dad, "I hope none of you daft beggars shot a dog," but of course there isn't any of them would do that; just Bram they would have shot.

Then our Dad sends them round again where they'd been before, and he picked our Lizbie up and carried her to a lear and I followed on and he put us in the hay and told us to stop there because this was a fight on and they weren't off to let any of Paterson folk out while they kept our Jane Ann.

So after a bit I went to sleep, and Lizbie too, and when we woke in the morning it was raining and there wasn't any breakfast or owt while our Dad and Tommy John came by and took us home and we fetched in the cows and milked and made a basket with tea and such, like it was drinkings for haytimers. We all came back after, both ways across the lake in our boat, and when we'd been gone the Copstone Gill lads had milked out Paterson cows but just on the ground, not to let the cows harm.

"There's nobody in the house," says Billy Mecca. "I've listened at all the windows on the ground. It's empty."

"Then we've won," says our Dad. "They'll have to give in."

"We've lost," says the Doctor. "You canna win over nowt. Or maybe we shot 'em all dead."

"Nay," says our Dad, "they're no good shot dead." But after that the Copstone Gill lads had a look in the house, and there's no one there but broken glass.

"They've gone," says Billy Mecca. "They'd gone before thou'd gotten here, Rich."

"Then they'll come back beaten," says our Dad. "There's no other place for them to go."

"Except maybe Scotland and a blacksmith wedding," says Billy. "What dost think to that?"

"Nay, but he brought the sheep down ready for clipping yesterday," says Dad. "He's off nowhere."

Lizbie says she'd rather marry a Scotchman, but they took no gaum of a bairn. But they decided that Bram will be back and maybe a few with him ready for a bonny fight, and they think they'll fight back grandly themselves, and

just will maybe wait and be ready.

They were right We'd had our dinners a good while, and it was on to milking time, and the two lads were slipping off up the pasture to bring Paterson cows on down when Bram came up the lane and stopped a way down.

"Rich Armistead," he shouted, calling of our Dad, "come by off our land and out of our yard, or by God I'll come in for thee."

46

"Nay, but we've getten hold on the spot and here we'll stop," our Dad shouts back. "While you give back our lass."

"Never," shouts Bram. "Not while the bells ring: never."

"Then we's here while the bells ring," says our Dad, "and come closer and we'll shoot ye."

But Bram hasn't come alone, and next thing I know is there's a fellow in the lear with me and Lizbie, but she doesn't know it's not one of ours, and he cares nowt for us but goes up on the balks and looks from the forking hole.

"Now, lad," he says, when I went up beside him," keep dark, or maybe there'll be a bat or two drop on you." But I saw from there the Copstone lad up by the cows get himself trapped in a corner and tied up, but he gave the fellows that got him a bunch or two first off.

Then there's some stones flung in the yard, and there's our Dad with two of them on him, and he cracked them together and they drop him.

Then there's a vast of whistles getting blown all round, and it's police whistles, and there were bobbies all over the spot, and they were taking no sides but they lock them all up in chains, like, handcuffs, all in a line together, and the man that came in with us went away down the wall and got himself caught and then it was all quiet.

Then there was a black van out in the lane and they

all got in, and they never put the chains on me and Lizbie. But they took our long gun and the brass cartridges Lizbie had.

Next there was our Jane Ann with Mrs Paterson and they were in a pony trap, and we were that glad to see Jane Ann we never minded we were in the trap with Mrs Paterson. But she was a right nice woman and we knew her anyroad. We went down with them to Hawes and then our Dad and Bram and them all got locked up in prison and Mrs Paterson she sobbed and sighed and had some gin, and Jane Ann she laughed and cried and we went to stop in a house there the night and got put to bed, and nobody to go out and feed Jem our dog or milk the cows.

SIX

It wasn't oft I wakened out of my own bed, and it was
right queer without our Lizbie, but she's getten in some
other bed. I looked from the window in that house and
there was such a clatterment of folk in the street and I
don't know what they're doing, but their clog irons were
at it on the stone, and some on them looking like Sunday,
and that was the shopkeepers getting to their shops and
having them open, and I wondered if I'd get a penny, but
I thought it might be a farthing and then I thought that
wasn't quite likely because they take away all your brass
in prison where they put our Dad.

50

Bram Paterson mother come and get me out then, and it was just a house to live in they had there, nowt going off like farming, and sour of soap and that, not milk and fire and our Dad pipe. There was breakfast on the kitchen table, but I'd not getten the cows in to milk this morning, and not the night before, and that wasn't right, because we'd milked Bram's cows and owt of that wanting done.

"Nay, Kitty, sit and eat," says our Jane Ann, and there she was like it was her house. "The cows got milked last night when all you men was laiking on the other side of the lake; and this morning let them bide a bit while we see what goes off with our Dad and all them."

"Them's all locked up," I says, and I thought it was true, locked up is for ever. "Thou must come away home, Jane Ann, and help us fend, because Lizbie's over little to keep house if I farm." I wasn't right fretted about our Dad, just with what there was to do at home. I knew he could do nowt bad, so there was no shame him getting locked up.

But Mrs Paterson looked aquart at that. "Does he only think his own way always?" she says to Jane Ann. "That's an old-farrand road for his mind to travel."

"Like his Dad," says our Jane Ann. "Isn't tha?"

"Nowt no worse for that," I says; and Mrs Paterson says what do I rightly think now, straight on, and I says I wondered about the cows first off, and then whether I might get a farthing to spend. So Mrs Paterson gave me a basin of oatmeal and some milk with the cream on it yet, and I wondered how they made butter.

I never got a farthing. In a bit we went out. Mrs Paterson says we can't take the bairns, but they had to take us for Lizbie clarped on our Jane Ann like tar, Jane Ann says, and we all went. There was a lot of folk; there was all the ones that came to our spot, and our Dad, and there was Black Bram and some that went with him, and there was plenty of policemen, and all the men had their hands fast in chains and all the bobbies had their painted sticks out.

"That's for if they make a carry-on," says Jane Ann. "Then it's tapping time."

We all went in the market hall, the old one, not what they have now and we all got spained off from the men like lambs get taken from the yowes, and there wasn't plenty of chairs so we stood up, and Jane Ann still carried our Lizbie.

I know what happened, for I've heard since, but there wasn't owt for me to see then, and not much I got to understand. I was all packed out with folk all round and all I heard was them chuntering at yon end the room. But first we got told to stand up, but we could do nowt to that but stop as we were.

Then a fellow read out like a parson or minister a long rigmarole about all these bad things the accused had done, and there was forever of names told, like Richard Armistead and Abraham Paterson and Christopher Awling, and Tan Hill Jack that has another name a-Sundays, but they never said our Jane Ann that was the bottom of the trouble.

They went back and forth with these names, and I leaned on Mrs Paterson while they ended, and there was one fellow for having them all cast back in prison and another for saying there was worse to come. But they hadn't the say; it wasn't any of them was the gaffer. The gaffer told them at last.

"I've heard plenty," he says. "I can't get it dealt with here; it has to come to court yet again for I doubt we've not heard the last of all you did wrong."

"Can we say nowt?" says Bram.

"Aye, speak out, lad," says Mrs Paterson.

"We'll have silence below there, madam," says the gaffer, "and no, you don't get to say a word now that'd be any use, for I won't let you, you might say wrong and it sounds as if you have got wrong enough already."

It doesn't seem right they should get in trouble and not be able to say, for when I'd to be in trouble our Dad would let me say my side of the job. But anyroad, it came out right for the time, when he says he'll let them all go if they've never done owt wrong before. It seemed they never had but for Doctor, and that wasn't bad enough for them to keep him then, just some tale about a licence. So they all got to go, but they were not to get themselves together any time any more than usual. "I am only letting you out to get on with your farming," he says. "I don't know what would become of all the stock if I didn't, but you've to respect mercy, for I shouldn't do it you've been so bad. So gan off to your homes and behave, else."

Jane Ann put Lizbie down on me, and she and Mrs Paterson cleared out and Lizbie bauled a bit and maybe I did and all, and then all the folks that were stood up had to stand again, and then they went, and there was just me and Lizbie while they came to lock up the market hall

54

and the woman put us out in the street.

Then our Dad found us, and he was rubbing his wrists, and by, he was twined with himself, and I've heard him call Jem our dog some of the words but not us bairns or hisself, so he must have been feeling badly.

"Well," he says at last, "I've getten loosed for now, so we'll just step on home and then. Did you see our Janey?"

"She holded me," says Lizbie. "Will she not be at home?"

"Not this turn about, I doubt," says Dad. "We haven't mannished the business yet. But thou ride like a jockey on my back, Lizbie, and we'll trot on nicely."

I think we trotted on about as fast as I could go, and it wasn't full rate, for after a time Bram came up after us and went up off the trod and through the ling and passed us and never turned his head.

"We got our breakfast at his mother house," says I.

"Well, think on thy dinner instead," says our Dad. "It'll keep thee filled longer that way," but we never got our dinner while teatime with milking and butter to make and eggs to bring in and what-all else.

And after, when we had done tea and our Dad went away up on top to look at the sheep, Lizbie and I went down on the lake side and looked over yonder to see whether Jane Ann might be there.

She stopped out of sight, but Black Bram himself came down the pasture yon side and got in our reed boat that was left there and rowed it over. He must have seen our Dad go off up the fellside. He rowed straight over to our landing and called of us, and he stopped in the boat and we stopped on land.

"There's nowt from me," says Bram. "But she sent summat over for you."

"Our Jane Ann?" says I.

"Aye," says he, "our Jane Ann. Take hold of the boat rope and I'll be off.'

So I got the boat rope, and Bram stepped out in the water and swam off, and I got the boat fast to the landing. Jane Ann sent us a big bread-loaf and some green bacon.

"What for did he bring yon?" says Lizbie.

Of course I couldn't take it home, or our Dad would go hairless. "It's nowt but some stones for the rabbits," says I, and when we came to the warreny place I put them down in a big hole, for not daring to let our Dad see them; and Lizbie dropped plenty more stones down the same places and I hoped she would say nowt when our Dad came back.

He just never made out where Jem our dog got this piece of fat bacon next day.

SEVEN

Our Jane Ann herself bobbed in one day when Dad was
at market. "Whisht," she says, "and not a word of I've
been here. By, what a scrow, and he wouldn't take any
gaum of it, would he? Well, I'll get it sided by and maybe
you'll see the floor. Now come by, our Lizbie, I isn't a
play-toy."

"Where's Bram at, then?" I says.

"At market just the same," says Jane Ann. "But don't
you let on to either on 'em that I was here, mind."

"Why don't you stop home a bit?" I says. "Or why
don't me and Lizbie come and stop wi' thee and Bram
Paterson mother?"

"Thou take out this stobbed rug and bray it with a stick," she says. But she hasn't answered me, and I went on a bit, for here she was and our Lizbie thought she was to stay for ever again same as she always did. "Now, Kitty," Jane Ann says at last, "it doesn't work out that road: they'd neither on 'em have it; and it doesn't work out the road it is, neither, and that's the top and bottom of it," and then she clattered me out with the rug and I hung it over a wall and brayed it with a stick the same as she said.

Then she went, flighted off. I wondered why she didn't get wed to Bram straight off but I'd no one to ask but Jem and he heard plenty and I hoped he never spoke, even if I did want an answer. I have over many shaffling little thoughts to let the whole world hear.

One day there came a letter and I had to go up for our Dad in Fairy Haw for him to write on the paper that came with it. When he got it open he shook his head and he shook it, and then he went to his money box and got out his gold money.

"I've to pay," he says. "I've to pay for the fettling of them windows at Paterson's, and such things. And I doubt this brass is never to be putten back. But, Kitty, it's all maybe gone astray with me this time, but thou promise never to give in if thou knows thou is right."

"I isn't right so very oft," I says.

"Thou will be," he says. "And we shall make a man of thee yet. Now I's off to get this account paid or there will be worse to follow. This letter's bad enough, but there's another, and maybe thou'lt ha' to be the man."

So off he went, and I thought I was to be a man in the do at Paterson's, but all it was I had more work after round the place, and the half of that was lasses' work at the fire side and such.

When he came back we got hungry. He'd brass neither to spend nor borrow and we hadn't bread. Our Jane Ann came over when we didn't always see her and put bread in the crock, and our Dad would never touch it, but he let me and Lizbie at it.

"Go to her if you want," he says. "I's not company, and maybe you'll be without me for a bit if the court goes far again us."

"I doubt she isn't happy yonder," I says, the plain road words come out and you don't know before what's in your mind. "We'll stop at home."

"But it's a dowly do, is home," he says, but he stirred up the peat fire and had us on his knees a bit and you might never know there was a Jane Ann.

The letter came to bid him to the police court again. After it came he sat by the fire all of the night, I believe, every night nearly, and by day when he set off to get at his work he would get in the yard and fetch up at a standstill and not know what to do, and I did all with Lizbie, and if it wasn't for bread and stuffs being on the bink by the dairy door of a morning there'd have been nowt to eat. That was Jane Ann.

The day he had to go we walked on together, like market day. On the bridge at the lake foot he turned round and saw all the farm out by the water. "Well," he says, "it's a bonny day to leave it on, with the leaves falling from the trees. I'll not come this way tonight, belike. But I stick by what I say: Bram Paterson shan't wed our lass if I have owt to say, and I have the say-so for years yet, while she gets to twenty one, and that stays whether I get in prison or not."

So we went on without looking back, and came to the court in good time and waited outside the door a while until a bobby came to lead him off another way, and he gave us a kiss in front of all the folk and left us. But Jane

60

Ann and Mrs Paterson came up with us then and took us in and this time we had a form to sit on, and when he said to stand then we could, so that was right.

Now then, it was a catechism going off that day, and they could every one have been at summat better. It didn't rightly take a day to tell what our Dad and them others had done, and we could have told them any time. I know they talked of the guns they had and they were

all off course about who fired the first one, and I'd done that with our duck-gun. Then they had the guns in and laughed a bit over Alice John's, and they couldn't reckon up the duck-gun to any of them before I told Mrs Paterson I did it and she told a bobby and he told the magistrate. So I got taken up there and given questions about telling the truth, and then I said a prayer to say the truth and I did, and I hoped I'd be in the prison with our Dad. But they sent me back to Jane Ann.

It turned out Paterson's was empty when our lot landed up there, and when the duck-gun went off they thought it was Bram shooting them. But Bram just walked up and saw what was going off and came back in town and got up his own lot to fight back. That was wrong, the police thought, because he should have gone to them and they would have done the job; but they got wit of it some road or other and sent down for men and came up after Bram to where we were, and Bram was locked in with the others.

So then we had dinner, and we heard a bobby say they were as good as hanged and they'd be locked up again sharp, but we took no account of him for we knew he came from Northallerton and what would he know?

Then we all got back in the room again after dinner, and the gaffer told us what he decided, and he's the law. He was a justice of the peace, he says, and the peace had been broken right badly and he wondered how long he should put them in prison, the pack of them. Then he says he thought better of it, when he looked at nineteen men and thought he would be spoiling nineteen farms, and he thought it would be best if all the accused got bound over. I thought he meant like tying down a pike for a windy night, but he meant that Dad and Bram and the Copstone Gill lads and Tan Hill Jack, and them all, were tied down to be good for their lives after, and not to get wrong even a lile bit. And our Dad and Bram he got severe with and said they'd neither of them to tread in each other land or liberty or in the lanes up to the houses or meet on other folk lands, only in the highway, and if that gets broken there'd be a bit of whistling. So the end dropped out of it and nowt came after all; they walked off and the down-country bobbies shook their heads, and the gaffer called on the next case.

That wasn't long coming. Bram and his people never said a word for themselves all day, but had a little man to speak for them, a lawyer. He bobs up then and started talking about our Jane Ann, and it seemed our Dad was wrong if he says Jane Ann can't wed Bram without his saying so, for there's this lawyer asking the Justice to say so instead of our Dad, but our Dad was there and this was getting asked over his head.

"What do you say, Richard Armistead?" says the Justice.

"I'd rather have getten in prison than said yes," said Dad. "That lass is seventeen and a half, and Bram Paterson

63

has getten to my age, and I reckon it's over-late for him to begin and over soon for her. And I won't give my consent to her getting wed to Bram, no, not while the bells ring."

"I know nothing about bells," says the justice. "But it seems to me that until a few tempers cool down, and until you are more settled up here in the dale, it would be better for me not to interfere. I put this application off until another day, and that will be the young lady's eighteenth birthday, which is next April, I believe. Thank you, gentleman."

Then he had his next case, and I don't know what it was, and we got out in the street again and Jane Ann walked off smartly and straight to the house there, and our Dad came for us. We walked back home, and that was a strange time, for I had Lizbie to carry and our Dad could hardly walk, being all of a dindle and sitting in the road as we went on and talking of what a trick of Bram's to pull on top of it all.

We came on home, and the fire was still burning, and you would think our Dad had been away from forever, going round and seeing all our old house rubbish as if he forgot it all during the day. But it comes on late and we have to get and call the cows in and milk them, the same as ever; and over the lake there's Bram doing the same; and I thought most part was forgotten and would right itself, soon, not when the bells rang.

EIGHT

We got away better at the back-end when our lambs were a good price at market and we sold two beasts, so for brass we were righter at the year-end than in the beginning. Our Dad brightened up too, and I heard him do what he hadn't done in a long time, sing a bit when he worked. He always says he sang no better than a raven.

There was a lot of fine fat feed in our pastures right to the time we took in the cows for winter, so on good days we let them out to graze again.

Our Dad had some word from folk about me and Lizbie, and how he had to keep us betterways. Before, when Jane Ann went, he let us be as we were, but I began to get ahead of what I had to wear, and Lizbie came out of

E

her dress just about altogether, and the weather getting colder we began to know. One market day our Dad tells us to stand there while he gets his hair clipped. But when he'd gone Jane Ann found us and took us along the stalls.

"We've to stop here," I says. "He's just off to see a clipper."

"Away," says Jane Ann, "did he not tell you? Why, I've to buy clothes for the pair of you, you're that bare of them like a hedge in winter."

It was all one to Lizbie what she wore, and not much different for me, but I came out of the market knowing I went in ragged, more than I knew when I had gone in; and Lizbie looked right smart.

"And there's just this," says Jane Ann, and she gave over a paper. "It's the bill."

"He won't like that," I says, because he never liked the bill for mending Paterson house. And I was right, and I was wrong. Jane Ann took us back on our corner and we waited while Dad came for us, and I gave him the paper and told him it was the bill.

"She needn't have troubled," he says. "You shall have what I can give, and I don't need the list of it." But when he opened the paper he got strong in the face and threw the writing down. "Well there," says he, "it's nobbut a letter from Bram, and if he was here I'd give it back the hard way."

But then he picks the paper up again and says, "Nay,

66

the world is different now and I've to be patient, and patience is right at last, whether I get locked up for not having it or not." And we went on home, and Lizbie was capped at the way she looked in the glass when we got there; and she got twined again when she pulled the parcel open we brought back, that just had in the old things. And that night he sat us on the kitchen table and clipped our hair with the sheep-clippers, and Lizbie's hair tumbled on the floor like light and mine was nowt, just shadows to hers.

"Now we look a gey bit better, all of us," he says. And he gathers up all that hair and drops it on the back of the fire, and he dropped that letter from Bram in with it. "It can say nowt," he says, and he kelked it down with the poker.

It did something for him, I think, and that was where he got the idea of writing a letter himself; and without remembering what happened to Bram's letter might happen to his; or maybe he thought it could never happen to his. He was several nights on the job, and it nearly came to nowt and landed on the back of our own fire. One day we came in from milking and it was one of those we all let on never happened, when Jane Ann would be over to tidy round and see about. Well, she'd had his letter out and gone over it and put his spellings right and that.

"Now, that's too saucy," says our Dad. "I wonder she didn't take it and deliver it all at the same time."

"She laughed a bit," says Lizbie. "And she cried a bit after, and then she went back yonder."

"I should go back yonder too and skelp her," says Dad. "But I've to think what I do these days, and it's hard on me. Well, I'll be daft to finish the letter," and he was about to throw it away when he thought he might be daft to do that and all, when Bram knew what it said. So he put it by. But he had it out again in a week or two. "It's a pity thou's no scholar neither, Kitty," he says. "You'll have to get put to school when the winter is over."

"Happen we'll write the letter then," I says, but he says he doesn't know what to say now and won't know what to say then.

Now this was back in the days before they had school boards and you weren't bound to go, but our Jane Ann had been, so I expected to. But I had some letters off Jane Ann, yet I could not then remember my name right through both parts.

We got wintered in. Jane Ann met us at market one day and had us fit some long leggings, and by, they kept out a lot of cold. Folk were all happed up and the ground got dried hard, and though we got our sheep down on the lake pastures there was no grass and we had to fother.

Night times the roof would crack and snap. Our Lizbie went and slept in Jane Ann bed a long time back, but she came in again with me and I could have done with Jem and all, for covers aren't so warm as sisters and animals.

One afternoon it came warmer just all of a sudden. Our Dad says he doesn't like it, and it's wintry enough already. But it wasn't wintry enough for the weather, and when we had our tea our Dad opened the door and let the light go out on the yard and there was snow coming down like it was clipping time yonder, coming down in flags and lying and joining up in a big white paving.

It snew the night through and it froze hard. But there were warm spots, like the shippon at milking time with the cows chewing and slopping and the milk cracking in the pail and coming in the dairy with hairy ice round the rim; and the stable with our horse Sugar in was warm, and the fire in the house. But nowhere else.

And there was always this aske wind, that never stopped. Most of the time it blew gentle, but there were days when it hurried on through our gates like the dog was on it, and the snow was stouring and banking up.

One day we went up with the sledge and Sugar to the lear in Grain Sike for a load of hay. I was nithered forking it down, and Sugar was nithered, and our Dad said his feet were like stones. I looked out in the wind and got great blebs of tears on my eyes off it, and I could see our road up blowing over already, and I saw our smoke at home, and there was Bram Paterson smoke yon side. But between all was white, and that place where there were no walls, that was Vendale Water, that was the lake, and there was snow right across it.

"Lake's frozen," I says.

"Aye," says our Dad. "I fothered the sheep in the west lake pasture and I wondered why it had getten so large. It was the ice growing out from the shore. Is it snow right over?"

I looked, and maybe there was a bit that was water yet,

but you could jump it, I says.

"Nay," says our Dad, "thou would be through the ice before thou'd getten so far. It takes a bad freeze to make all hard."

In a week it was a bad freeze. Dad could tell, when our dog went across that way on his visits when he mostly trotted round the foot of the lake.

"He's welcome to cross," said our Dad. "But you stop off it, Kitty and Lizbie; once you've getten in that water you'll come out dead, so do you hear?"

I wanted to know if someone would tell our Jane Ann, and our Dad says Bram knows, and he'd trust him with that.

That night after tea he said he had a thought, by God, and there was nowt could be done about it by anyone, Justice of the Peace or not, and he got out the letter he started and this time he tore the paper off and threw it in the fire.

"I know what to say now," he said, "and sithee, they can do nowt about it. There's Bram and me wanting the same thing all this while, that we got spoiled of before, and that's a fight, and a good fight too, to settle all, and the winner to have his way: if I win our lass comes back and no more said, and if he wins she can wed him, and Black Bram and I come a fair match, so the winner is the one that wants his way the most, and that's Rich Armistead, for I'll not believe Bram has less spite than love.

71

And we shan't either of us get off our own lands and liberties, but we shan't get on the other's. I'll make a fair offer, and he can't back off."

So the offer got made, and it kept the law the gaffer gave at the police court, for they would not meet on either's lands, or on any others', and not in a highway either, but they would have the fight out on the ice of the lake, just at the mid place.

Our Dad could not trust this letter with the postman, for word might get out. So he walked with me down to the bridge, and I walked up yon side with it, and there was Bram mucking out the stable. I gave him the letter.

"Aye," he said. "We'll do it tomorrow in the afternoon. The weather will hold. And we'll get all ended, Kitty. You tell him tomorrow after dinner, out in the middle, bare-handed."

NINE

"Daft, daft, daft," says our Jane Ann, or shouts it just as she came in the door next morning.

"Thou's speaking, then?" says our Dad.

"I's not," says Jane Ann, "nobbut calling thee a daft fool, and him yonder and all."

"It isn't worth doing owt to please thee," says Dad. "We'll not be right whatever. So happen we're off to please ourselves, me and Bram."

"I wouldn't stop either of you great bairns," says Jane Ann. "The pair of you can do as you please, and I's not bound to take notice of the winner, there's no choosing between gauvies."

"No," says our Dad. "Thou's not bound. But Bram is, seest thou; and thou will see it was just a fancy you have, either of you."

"It never is," says Jane Ann. "I'll wed him yet; but loss him or not I'll not come back here no road."

"Thou'll be here first thing, belike," says our Dad. "Thou is now."

Then she goes off in a hig, but not before she took a look in the dairy, at all the cheese and butter and what wasn't curdled before was soured then by the look on her, worse than a black slug.

"I can't give backward," says our Dad, when she has gone. "But I hadn't aimed to get her stirred up so."

The day wasn't so cold, with the wind dropping and the air stood still, and it was a wonder so much cloud was in the sky, not a gap open all day, and all right dark so we had a candle on the table at dinner. There was summat on the road for us, our Dad says, and even Lizbie thought it was demming in for something and put her doll in bed.

It was so still I could hear them across the lake at Paterson's, where our Jane Ann had them tied, Bram and his mother, and I had no need to hear the words, and I was right glad she was yonder for when she took a turn like that she would round on anyone for owt or nowt. There was our horse making quiet noises in the stable, and the cows nattling their chains on the redsters, and coughing, and it was like the day stopped before it got right up, darky and calm as it was.

Then there was a strange noise, and I couldn't tell whether it was miles off or just a buzz in my ears. Our

Dad says he could maybe hear it, he wasn't sure and wouldn't be troubled, because just now he was setting out what to wear at the fight. He reckoned trousers and a waistcoat would be best, no shirt for the sleeves to catch, no kerchief, and socks and boots, or maybe foot-cloths and clogs, he's not sure. But he was stitching up his pockets so Bram wouldn't get a hold on them, so I left him.

Lizbie never said whether she heard the sound, but she said, "Wash thysen, muckylugs."

But it was there, and maybe it was the sea, the day was so still the sound might come over the fells. I went out again and I knew I heard it, because yon side there was Bram and Mrs Paterson and Jane Ann and they stood and listened.

Then it got so dark the clock must be wrong. Our Dad was fit to go, but he wondered, and then he took a lantern, "or Bram won't see I've set off," he says. "Now you just keep the fire up and we'll have tea when I land back; and maybe Janey with it. So thee stop at home, Kitty."

Of course I wasn't off to stop at home and never let the door close but followed out after, out in that strange rustling noise so far off, and there's our Dad in front with the lantern burning near red, and then Jem our dog following just after, and me at the back, and down the hillside yonder there walked another light, and that was Bram.

And I was thinking, our Dad's bigger than Bram, like more thick across so I hope he wins; but that won't be so good for Jane Ann; so I hope he loses, but that's not so good for him, and I have to be on either side at once and I can't. So I padded on behind and when our Dad came to our landing he stepped down on the ice, and waited for Bram to come off the hill yon side and walked out to him.

I stepped down on the ice in turn, and the wind has taken most of the snow off and I can feel the reeds clamped up through the ice, and I stood among them and waited to see how they went out there.

When the lantern got further away it was easier to see what was doing: nearhand it filled my eyes too much. So I saw Bram and him meet and talk a bit, and then they stepped aside and set the lanterns down. I couldn't make out what they said to one another, but I heard the next bit, which was our Dad telling Jem to sit and drop flat and Bram saying the same to Bess, and both dogs got away by and dropped flat.

Then there was quiet for a bit, but for the sound like the sea far off.

"Thou can walk off now, Bram," says our Dad. "Nowt no worse."

"I'll walk off after," says Bram, "I isn't flayd." Then they go on with the tongue-fight a bit, at each other with bad words, and Jem gets up and barks, and they turned on him together and sat him down again, and went on.

They never got to grips, just went on gingering each

76

other up ready for the first bazzock, give or take. There they were, muttering and cursing, and there's that sound like reeds rattling, louder now, and then there's both dogs up and making a whimper and sniffing the ice, I think.

Then all of a clap there was a great noise like a gun but even brighter and sharper, and I could not tell where it came from, and it echoed back round and round the lake, and I thought it was a gun and the police were coming to get them both. It set the dogs uneasy too, and they began to circle and Bram and Dad stood still. Then there was another of the reports, and the dogs ran for the shore. That noise banged back and forth too, and then went on, a rip-rap, crickle-crackle, and there was the surface of the lake moving in front of me, and the lanterns shaking about and then out they went, one and then the other. But I could see well enough without them, and what I saw was Bram and our Dad not there any more.

I thought they were down fighting under a bank of snow, because I did see an arm lift and maybe a head raised. But then there was a call out from the middle and something lifted that wasn't an arm or a head or any part of a man, but a white thing, and I am thinking of huge fish maybe we forgot about, and then I knew it was a great tip-over of ice, lifted like half a garth and fallen down again slap on water, and I heard that slap and after it no one called.

I ran out on the ice, and when I got out beyond the

77

reed-tops it was that slape I dropped down on my face, but I got up and went on.

I came on the ice where it wasn't soft, but you might think it was something like it, where it would give and lift again. That didn't stop me, and I knew I'd crossed a crack I hadn't seen. But the next crack I saw, where water was lifting in it and curdling on top just a little; and the crack after that was too big to cross and the next ice was shifting and on edge and laid up in ledges like a heap of flagstones.

I backed off and went round, and the next steps I took made cracks between my feet, and I heard them, and I went down again when my feet walked different ways, and stopped down for it was better to crawl, my knees held better.

I was crawling round where I saw something neither
ice nor water, but in one and under the other, and holding
on. It was my Dad, and Jane Ann's too, and she was on
the ice in her apron and making no better go than I was.
But we got round the broken place and together, and there
was Bram and our Dad together too, and holding each
other up, it seemed, but they were both like dead and
eyes closed and the ice had riven the skin off their arms
and heads and they trickled down with blood, and there
was the ice packing in again round them. And there we
had hold of them and we couldn't get them out of the
water, they were too heavy and too dead.

Mrs Paterson came dothering out with a stick she thought might come to be useful, and Jane Ann thought we might break a way to land with it, but it slipped off the edge of the ice and down into the water. But then it touched ground, and the water wasn't more than leg-deep, and before I could think Jane Ann stepped down into it and gave a great yell like being bitten and got her shoulder under Bram, because he was near, and hiked him up to me and Mrs Paterson, and then the same with our Dad, and then the same with herself.

"Bring them on the bank," she says. "I'll get our sledge," but she means Paterson sledge from that side, which is where we are by now, not our side at all.

Well, she dressed their horse any road at all, he was a sight, but she was back in a minute, by the time we were at the bank, pulling and pushing our two. And all the time there was the ice tinkering away and that grizzle of sound coming nearer, and then it turned to rain on us, and by, it was grateful and warm.

TEN

"There's neither of them drowned by the lake, but it's this rain that will choke them," says Jane Ann, but I could hardly hear her words she shuddered so with cold. But their horse Prince had the sledge pulled up their pasture and in their yard right sharp, with Mrs Paterson leading it and running, and I was there between them getting their hands up off the ground so the spurs the sledge goes on don't overrun them.

We got up again the back door and the yard was full of trodden snow and water lying on it so we can't much move easy. But there were three of us and we got them off the sledge one at a time and hauled in the kitchen and dropped on the floor.

F

Bram Paterson dog Bess came back then and looked foolish for running off, and got herself kicked out again and we won't listen to her story.

"We'll not stop while we've finished," says Jane Ann. "We'll ha' to get them up on a bed." That was not so bad a problem, because Mrs Paterson and her hoist them up by the armpits and trail them up the stairs first one and then the other and I ran on with a candle and to open the doors. We laid them on a big bed with the covers pulled back. Mrs Paterson says, "What's a bit of damp under 'em? Nowt. But you Jane Ann get away and doff them wet clothes, and find what you can in my press; and Kitty and I will get these two laid out proper and their clothes off: he's another man, is Kitty, and Bram I first saw nak'd, and Rich I've seen the bare bottom of many a time when he was swimming and that with Bram."

"If they're not quite dead," I says.

"Nooa," she says, "not by a long ways, just knocked silly, or maybe knocked sensible."

The boots came off hardest on the pair of them, and our Dad caused some trouble until we found he'd put a stitch top and bottom of his waistcoat buttons as well as sewing up the pockets. Mrs Paterson rived it apart. Then we dried them, and then we covered them, and Jane Ann brought in two stone bottles of hot water for their feet and wrapped them in a cloth and set them under the happings.

"And now," says Jane Ann, "what?"

"I'll make a cup of tea," says Mrs Paterson. "And you and Kitty set the fire in this room and warm it up."

There we sat down below, listening up to them but they never made a sound, and we supped our tea. Mrs Paterson lit up the oil lamp on the table.

Then I remembered Lizbie at home with just a fire and no light and maybe not even Jem, and I thought the rain might be frighting her out of her wits, and I was for off and get her, but we considered first, says Mrs Paterson, which should go, because any of us might, and it came to me at last. Then we looked out and it seemed no one could take a foot pace through all the slother and blathery stuff. But there was Prince there in the yard yet with all his gear sorry on him and the sledge at the back of him, and then I've no problem. I took a sack to cover me and a sack for Lizbie, got the most of the gear off Prince, and got up on his back, and I'd done that with our horses plenty of times.

We thought it was bad in the yard, but out beyond the gate it was worse, with a breeze coming under the rain, and out at the foot of the lake it was terrible with the wind coming down the lake, and I thought it had coldened up. But Prince went on and on and it never bothered him, over the bridge and his great foot sloshing down in the slippy stuff and sucking up when he lifted them, and water in his skin.

Then I thought of a load of things to get done when I was back, which was fodder the horse, milk the cows, sarra the fowls, but maybe leave the sheep a night, and they'd scrape down for grass in the morning. I went in to Lizbie first.

She was right enough, sat by the fire in the dark, so I got her some bread and treacle and had a bit myself and took the crust for Prince and he lapped off the treacle on my fingers. Then I got our other lantern and milked the cows and that, but I left the milk in the shippon because it would never carry over the ground as it was, and I'd to walk by the wall side to get summat to hold on.

Lizbie didn't want to get out from her fire, and I didn't want to either for comfort, but I had to know about our Dad, so I picked her up and put her up on Prince and she shrieked but he knew better than to take any gaum of that. Then I had to climb up on a gate cheek to get on myself, and we tramped back to the other side.

When we got down the foot of the lake it was bad as ever, or worse, belike, but a bit less rain and more wind, and we heard the ice all broken up and wrangling and dinging but I couldn't look that way in the wind even if it was day. We came up to Paterson's, and there's our dog trailed us all the way along grinning like he does, and watching him and one thing and another I dropped Lizbie of in the puddles and there was a sing-song.

"Whisht," says Mrs Paterson at the door, and they tell

84

us when we got in that Bram woke up but said nowt, and then swooned off or went to sleep, they don't know which it was. But our Dad was still brayed silly by the lump of ice I saw rise and fall, I reckon. But for now Mrs Paterson doesn't want Bram wakened.

She put Lizbie and me down again the fire to dry out, for there's nowt for us to change to. Then she and Jane Ann went out and milked and sike things, just as I'd done. And we by the fire were on nurse-guard, and I dreaded most the policeman to come and find our Dad the wrong side of the lake and get him locked up.

Then we had our proper tea, and went to bed, and the rain lashed and the wind blustered outside and whummered in a chimney and got under the linoleum in that room and like walked about so I kept waking to it.

In the morning the rain had gone and the wind dropped down a bit, and outside the green grass showed itself through, and I saw our sheep fending and finding beyond the lake, and the lake itself was all flags of ice jinkling and jauping and rising and floating and batting on one another so it clattered our ears and Mrs Paterson kept looking on her delf rack to see if the cups hung up were jostling each other.

Bram waked in the morning, and I was there. He made to move but he couldn't. "Ooah, mother," he says, "what have I getten? I can hardlings breathe," and he turned his head just a little and a little and saw there was another in

the bed with him. "Who's yon?" he says, with not turning his head plenty.

"Rich," says Mrs Paterson.

"Is he dead?" says Bram.

"He's not, but he is bad," says Mrs Paterson. "But you'd be better if you could get up. Where does it pain you?"

"Everywhere," says Bram. "But win or lose, eh?"

"You never fought, you silly beggars," says Mrs Paterson.

"I'll mend, and then," says Bram. "But not yet awhile.

What's the weather?"

"Thawing," says Mrs Paterson. "Hear the ice blating on the lake."

"I thought it was my head," says Bram, and he drew up a hand to touch it and found it lapped in cloth.

"Lie easy," says Jane Ann then. "You've gotten banged and scratched, no more than that. But our Dad's knocked silly, and I don't know the bigger fool, the waker or the sleeper, two such fellows ligging in such a bed. You came in it nowt, one fish, two fish, and you'll maybe come out of it nowt." Then Bram asked for something to sup and went off to sleep again, or closed his eyes again his aching head. And Mrs Paterson says, "Nay, he was born in yon bed; it knows him."

Our Dad opened his eyes near dinner time, but he was daft as a brush and first off I thought he was acting it, but he still hadn't his wits. Mrs Paterson said they were all of a mashel yet and maybe he'd gotten his eyes open but that was all; he was still senseless. But he was talking on and trying to move, and he would just take a spoon of tea and another and on till the cup was empty so he wasn't clean crazy.

"Just banged on the head," says Jane Ann. "He might come out better than before, that one; but we'll never make owt of the other," and Bram says to her to wait on and he'll settle her.

By next morning Bram sat up and walked about. Our

Dad sat up and remembered in habs and nabs, now about the cows, and then about the police court, and looked for Jane Ann or Lizbie or me, or our mother, and then he wanted to know what the hymns were, and then not be late for school. Then he seemed full in his wits and says how his back hurts, and when would they get to stop ringing the bells.

"It was a sore thump he had," said Mrs Paterson. But I'd had no thump and I knew what he meant: there were the bells of the city under the lake ringing day and night, and what that might be was the ice chiming and jangling and singing, so now was the time the bells rang.

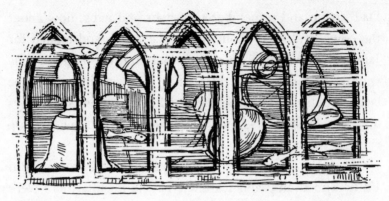

ELEVEN

I said nowt. Maybe I had only a silly fancy like our Dad;
or maybe I thought I'd not get a listen from them. So I
left it in my head, same as it was in his, but I listened to it
coming in my lugs all day and the next day too.

Our Dad went off back to sleep, the day he heard the
bells. I thought he was still knocked silly, but Mrs Paterson
says he sleeps healthily now and we aren't to worry.

We'd not much to worry. Jane Ann and I went over to
the farm twice in the day, and the third day we went in
the reed boat with all the ice gone. Bram hirpled about
lamely but he got his own work done, and Lizbie was
happiest of all, with Jane Ann for mother and Mrs Paterson
for gran and Bram for uncle.

Then the next day after we went across in the reed
boat our Dad woke in the morning, and I went in to him.

"My head aches," he says, "I think there's both our

90

horses in there getting shod; and my back's bad, and I don't know how I came here, and I want some breakfast: I's right, see thou."

He was right, but he wasn't better, says Mrs Paterson. He got his breakfast but no clothes so he stopped where he was. I told him how he came there, and he had forgotten the fight and most things until now, but he recalled thinking there could be a fight.

"So we'd getten into it, had we?" he says.

"Into the lake, that's all," I says. "And lost a lantern each."

"So there was no winner," he says.

"Thou had thy end knocked in longest," I says. "So if the fight had begun thou'd be the loser. Mrs Paterson says you're both losers."

"Well, I must get away," he says. "I've no right here by law, so I's bound to gan home."

However, he had a sleepy day or two yet of it, but he kept his wits. And Bram stopped out of the way, not knowing quite how they were friendly. But then they met, when our Dad got himself down the stairs and sat again the fire, dindly but better.

"Now, Rich," says Bram.

"Now, Bram," says Rich. "Is thou still fixed on wedding our lass?"

"Now Rich," says Bram, "that hasn't to come up between us for four month yet, and we aren't to be speaking together a word."

"Maybe I've to fight thee afresh," says our Dad.

Jane Ann came in right fast from the dairy. "Now get in separate rooms," she says. "You've to be apart, so do it or thou (and she waved a skimmer on our Dad) will get put back in bed. We's right as we are for now, and don't fret."

"Nay, I isn't fretting," says our Dad. "I made up my mind long since, and I'll bide by what I said, so come by, Janey, and set down yon skimmer or it'll be through the window."

But Jane Ann says she won't hear any more of it, and he's to behave. So he sat there and nodded his head a bit and says she's right and he'll say no more while he gets in his own house again.

We got back in our own house in a week, and he was right as owt, but for just one thing, he never seemed angered or put about. He would sing again to himself, like a crow, but he never sat again the fire and looked in it and rubbed his fingers together, and he wasn't so stiff by any means.

Jane Ann came over with us in our boat and Bram said he would come on over in their boat before milking time. But when that time was coming our Dad says to Jane Ann that she must stop a while longer, and he wants Bram up at the house.

So Bram comes up when he tires of waiting at the

landing. He came up ready for trouble with Jane Ann, thinking she might have settled to live at home now and he wouldn't know where that would lead.

"Sit thee down, Bram," says our Dad. "I've time for this before milking, and so has thou."

"I shouldn't be here," says Bram.

"Go if thou likes," says Dad. "Then sit, lad. This is what I said from the beginning about her and thee, that I'd not let her wed thee while I had the say-so, unless the bells rang, and you know what bells those are."

"There isn't any bells down below there," says Jane Ann. "You mean never, and what for do you repeat it?"

"Nay, but listen first," says our Dad. "I wasn't right out of my wits all the time there. I heard the bells ring on two days and two nights, I heard them clear."

"It would be dark to take advantage of thee, Rich," said Bram. "But there was no bells, only in thy head, man."

"That's what I thought," said our Dad, "but I heard it plenty of times then, and so did you, and all of us, but you never knew what it was."

So I bobbed in and said I heard it too, but Bram still says Nay, and Jane Ann thinks he's still knocked silly and takes no notice of me. Then Bram scratched his head.

"By God," he said, "thou's right, Rich. I heard it so mich I never gave it a thought. I heard the bells ringing a long time, day and night, and I never knew it, and so

did thou hear them too, Jane Ann, when the ice jankled and struck and played tunes.''

"Well," said Jane Ann, "I think I'm better at a tune than he is, so why did I not know what it was?''

"Thou never listened to me," says our Dad; "what for would you listen to that? Well, I heard the bells ring, and that was my word. Whether it came as a miracle or what I don't know, but I never heard it before in my life, and there it is, them old stories is true, and come summer Lizbie and I will be off to look for the roof tops too.''

94

"Well, I do wonder," says Jane Ann, "what was it I stood on when I pulled the two great lumps of ye out of the water?"

Then the poor cows got a late milking again, and the world will think we're no sort of farmers, for the three of them had a drink from our bottle and our Dad sung worse than a rook when he went to milking, and as for Bram, he couldn't row to the far side of the lake which is odd when the sides is the biggest bit, but he got moiled around in the centre, with our Dad shouting from one side and Mrs Paterson from the other.

They got wed just at Easter and Lizbie sucked her thumb at the back of Jane Ann through the service, and just at Christmas there's a baby for Lizbie to have for a play-toy when Jane Ann came over. Our Dad and Bram went and saw the Justice of the Peace at his own house, for him to say they can go on each other's land. So that haytime again we did the two garths together, and then Beldin and Delveland, but we did all together, mowing and turning and dashing and windrowing turn and turn about, and the same Irishman worked in with us, and so through Fairy Haw and the rest. And I'll end when our Dad was right taken with the baby and just began to wonder whether it was time to look round for himself again, for if Bram can then so can he and he hasn't decided about waiting while the bells ring.